THIS IS A COFFEE TABLE BOOK

COFFEE TABLE ART

[Agency FB]

COFFEE

TABLE ART

[ALGERIAN]

COFFEE TABLE ART

[AR BERKLEY]

COFFEE TABLE ART

[AR Blanca]

COFFEE
TABLE ART

[AR BONNIE]

COFFEE

TABLE ART

[AR CARTER]

COFFEE TABLE ART

[AR CENA]

COFFEE
TABLE ART

[AR CHRISTY]

COFFEE
TABLE ART

[AR DARLING]

COFFEE TABLE ART

[AR DECODE]

COFFEE TABLE ART

[AR DELANEY]

COFFEE TABLE
ART

[AR DESTINE]

COFFEE TABLE ART

[AR ESSENCE]

COFFEE TABLE

ART

[AR HERMANN]

COFFEE
TABLE ART

[AR JULIAN]

COFFEE TABLE ART

[Arial]

COFFEE TABLE ART

[Arial Black]

COFFEE TABLE ART

[Arial Narrow]

COFFEE TABLE ART

[Arial Rounded MT Bold]

COFFEE TABLE

ART

[AvenirLT-Medium]

COFFEE TABLE ART

[AvenirLT-Roman]

COFFEE TABLE ART

[Bahnschrift]

COFFEE TABLE ART

[Bahnschrift Condensed]

COFFEE TABLE ART

[Bahnschrift Light]

COFFEE TABLE ART

[Bahnschrift Light Condensed]

COFFEE TABLE ART

[Bahnschrift Light SemiCondensed]

COFFEE
TABLE ART

[Bahnschrift Light SemiBold]

COFFEE TABLE ART

[Bahnschrift Light SemiBold Condensed]

COFFEE TABLE ART

[Bahnschrift Light SemiBold SemiCondensed]

COFFEE TABLE ART

[Bahnschrift SemiCondensed]

COFFEE
TABLE ART

[Bahnschrift SemiLight]

COFFEE TABLE ART

[Bahnschrift SemiLight Condensed]

COFFEE TABLE
ART

[Bahnschrift SemiLight SemiCondensed]

COFFEE TABLE ART

[Basekerville Old Face]

COFFEE TABLE ART

[Bahaus 93]

COFFEE
TABLE ART

[Bell MT]

COFFEE TABLE ART

[Berlin Sans FB]

COFFEE TABLE ART

[Berlin Sans FB Demi]

COFFEE TABLE

ART

[Bernard MT Condensed]

COFFEE

TABLE

ART

[Blackadder ITC]

COFFEE TABLE ART

[Bodoni MT]

COFFEE TABLE ART

[Bodoni MT Black]

COFFEE TABLE ART

ART

[Bodoni MT Condensed]

COFFEE TABLE ART

[Bodoni MT Poster Condensed]

COFFEE
TABLE ART

[Book Antiqua]

COFFEE
TABLE ART

[Bookman Old Style]

COFFEE TABLE ART

[Bradley Hand ITC]

COFFEE TABLE ART

[Britannic Bold]

COFFEE TABLE ART

[Broadway]

COFFEE TABLE ART

[Brush Script MT]

COFFEE TABLE ART

[Calibri]

COFFEE TABLE ART

[Calibri Light]

COFFEE TABLE ART

[Californian FB]

COFFEE TABLE ART

[Calisto MT]

COFFEE

TABLE ART

[Cambria]

COFFEE TABLE ART

[Cambria Math]

COFFEE TABLE ART

[Candara]

COFFEE TABLE

ART

[Candara Light]

COFFEE TABLE ART

[CASTELLAR]

COFFEE TABLE ART

[Centaur]

COFFEE
TABLE ART

[Century]

COFFEE TABLE ART

[Century Gothic]

COFFEE
TABLE ART

[Century Schoolbook]

COFFEE TABLE

ART

[Chiller]

COFFEE TABLE ART

[Colonna MT]

COFFEE TABLE ART

[Comic Sans MS]

COFFEE
TABLE ART

[Consolas]

COFFEE
TABLE ART

[Constantia]

COFFEE TABLE ART

[Cooper Black]

COFFEE TABLE

ART

[Copperplate Gothic Bold]

COFFEE TABLE ART

[Copperplate Gothic Light]

COFFEE
TABLE ART

[Corbel]

COFFEE
TABLE ART

[Corbel Light]

COFFEE
TABLE ART

[Courier New]

COFFEE TABLE

ART

[Curlz MT]

COFFEE TABLE ART

[Ebrima]

COFFEE TABLE ART

[Edwardian Script ITC]

COFFEE

TABLE ART

[ELEPHANT]

COFFEE TABLE ART

[ENGRAVERS MT]

COFFEE
TABLE ART

[Eras Bold ITC]

COFFEE
TABLE ART

[Eras Demi ITC]

COFFEE
TABLE ART

[Eras Light ITC]

COFFEE TABLE ART

[Eras Medium ITC]

COFFEE TABLE ART

[FELIX TITLING]

COFFEE TABLE

ART

[Fontdinerdotcom Sparkly]

COFFEE TABLE ART

[Footlight MT Light]

COFFEE TABLE ART

[Forte]

COFFEE TABLE ART

[Franklin Gothic Book]

COFFEE TABLE ART

[Franklin Gothic Demi]

COFFEE TABLE ART

[Franklin Gothic Demi Cond]

COFFEE TABLE ART

[Franklin Gothic Heavy]

COFFEE
TABLE ART

[Franklin Gothic Medium]

COFFEE
TABLE ART

[Franklin Gothic Medium Cond]

COFFEE TABLE ART

[Freestyle Script]

COFFEE TABLE ART

[French Script MT]

COFFEE TABLE

ART

[Gabriola]

COFFEE
TABLE ART

[Gadugi]

COFFEE TABLE ART

[Garamond]

COFFEE
TABLE ART

[Georgia]

COFFEE
TABLE ART

[Gigi]

COFFEE TABLE ART

[Gill Sans MT]

COFFEE TABLE
ART

[Gill Sans MT Condensed]

COFFEE TABLE ART

[Gill Sans MT Ext Condensed Bold]

COFFEE TABLE ART

[Gill Sans Ultra Bold]

COFFEE TABLE ART

[Gill Sans Ultra Bold Condensed]

COFFEE TABLE ART

[Gloucester MT Extra Condensed]

COFFEE TABLE

ART

[Goudy Old Style]

COFFEE

TABLE ART

[Goudy Stout]

COFFEE TABLE ART

[Haettenschweller]

COFFEE TABLE
ART

[Harlow Solid Italic]

COFFEE TABLE ART

[Harrington]

COFFEE
TABLE ART

[High Tower Text]

COFFEE TABLE ART

[HoloLens MDL2 Assets]

COFFEE TABLE ART

[Impact]

COFFEE TABLE ART

[Imprint MT Shadow]

COFFEE TABLE ART

[Informal Roman]

COFFEE TABLE ART

[Ink Free]

COFFEE

TABLE ART

[Javanese Text]

COFFEE TABLE ART

ART

[Jokerman]

COFFEE TABLE ART

[Juice ITC]

COFFEE TABLE ART

[Kristen ITC]

COFFEE TABLE ART

[Kunstler Script]

COFFEE
TABLE ART

[Leelawadee]

COFFEE
TABLE ART

[Leelawadee UI]

COFFEE TABLE ART

[Leelawadee UI Semilight]

COFFEE
TABLE ART

[Lucida Bright]

COFFEE TABLE ART

ART

[Lucida Calligraphy]

COFFEE TABLE ART

ART

[Lucida Console]

COFFEE TABLE ART

[Lucida Fax]

COFFEE TABLE

ART

[Lucida Handwriting]

COFFEE
TABLE ART

[Lucida Sans]

COFFEE
TABLE ART

[Lucida Sans Typewriter]

COFFEE TABLE ART

[Lucida Sans Unicode]

COFFEE TABLE ART

ART

[Magneto]

COFFEE TABLE ART

[Maiandra GD]

COFFEE

TABLE ART

[Malgun Gothic]

COFFEE TABLE

ART

[Malgun Gothic Semilight]

COFFEE TABLE ART

[Matura MT Script Capitals]

COFFEE TABLE ART

[Microsoft Himalaya]

COFFEE

TABLE ART

[Microsoft JhengHei]

COFFEE
TABLE ART

[Microsoft JhengHei Light]

COFFEE

TABLE ART

[Microsoft JhengHei UI]

COFFEE

TABLE ART

[Microsoft JhengHei UI Light]

COFFEE
TABLE ART

[Microsoft New Tai Lue]

COFFEE
TABLE ART

[Microsoft PhagsPa]

COFFEE
TABLE ART

[Microsoft Sans Serif]

COFFEE

TABLE ART

[Microsoft Tae Le]

COFFEE TABLE

ART

[Microsoft Uighur]

COFFEE
TABLE ART

[Microsoft YaHei]

COFFEE
TABLE ART

[Microsoft YaHei Light]

COFFEE

TABLE ART

[Microsoft YaHei UI]

COFFEE

TABLE ART

[Microsoft YaHei UI Light]

COFFEE TABLE ART

[Microsoft Yi Baiti]

COFFEE TABLE
ART

[MingLiU_HKSCS-ExtB]

COFFEE TABLE ART

[MingLiU-ExtB]

COFFEE
TABLE ART

[Mistral]

COFFEE
TABLE ART

[Modern No. 20]

COFFEE
TABLE ART

[Mongolian Baiti]

COFFEE TABLE
ART

[Monotype Corsiva]

COFFEE TABLE

ART

[MS Gothic]

□◆□ □□□□□□□□

COFFEE

TABLE ART

[MS PGothic]

COFFEE TABLE ART

[MS Reference Sans Serif]

COFFEE
TABLE ART

[MS UI Gothic]

COFFEE
TABLE ART

[MV Boli]

COFFEE

TABLE ART

[Myanmar Text]

COFFEE TABLE ART

[Niagara Engraved]

COFFEE TABLE ART

[Niagara Solid]

COFFEE
TABLE ART

[Nirmala UI]

COFFEE TABLE ART

ART

[Nirmala UI Semilight]

COFFEE TABLE
ART

[NSimSum]

COFFEE
TABLE ART

【OCR A Extended】

COFFEE TABLE

ART

[OCR B MT]

COFFEE TABLE ART

ART

[OCR-A II]

COFFEE
TABLE ART

[Old English Text MT]

COFFEE TABLE ART

[Onyx]

COFFEE TABLE

ART

[Palace Script MT]

COFFEE
TABLE ART

[Palatino Linotype]

COFFEE TABLE ART

[Papyrus]

[Parchment]

COFFEE
TABLE
ART

[Perpetua]

COFFEE TABLE ART

[Perpetua Titling mt]

COFFEE TABLE ART

[Playbill]

COFFEE
TABLE ART

[PMingLiU-ExtB]

COFFEE TABLE ART

ART

[Poor Richard]

COFFEE
TABLE ART

[Pristina]

COFFEE TABLE

ART

[QuickType II]

COFFEE TABLE

ART

[QuickType II Condensed]

COFFEE TABLE ART

[QuickType II Mono]

COFFEE TABLE ART

[Quick Type IIPi]

COFFEE TABLE ART

(Rage Italic)

COFFEE TABLE ART

ART

[Ravie]

COFFEE
TABLE ART

[Rockwell]

COFFEE
TABLE ART

[Rockwell Condensed]

COFFEE TABLE ART

[Rockwell Extra Bold]

COFFEE TABLE ART

[Script MT Bold]

COFFEE TABLE ART

[Segoe MDL2 Assets]

COFFEE TABLE ART

[Segoe Print]

COFFEE TABLE ART

[Segoe Script]

COFFEE TABLE ART

[Segoe UI]

COFFEE TABLE ART

[Segoe UI Black]

COFFEE TABLE ART

[Segoe UI Emoji]

COFFEE TABLE ART

[Segoe UI Historic]

COFFEE TABLE ART

[Segoe UI Light]

COFFEE TABLE ART

[Segoe UI SemiBold]

COFFEE TABLE ART

[Segoe UI SemiLight]

COFFEE TABLE ART

[Segoe UI Symbol]

COFFEE TABLE ART

ART

[Showcard Gothic]

COFFEE TABLE ART

[SimSun]

COFFEE TABLE
ART

[SimSun-ExtB]

COFFEE TABLE

ART

[Sitka Banner]

COFFEE TABLE ART

[Sitka Display]

COFFEE
TABLE ART

[Sitka Heading]

COFFEE
TABLE ART

[Sitka Small]

COFFEE TABLE ART

[Sitka Subheading]

COFFEE
TABLE ART

[Sitka Text]

COFFEE TABLE ART

ART

[Snap ITC]

COFFEE TABLE
ART

[STENCIL]

COFFEE TABLE ART

[Sylfaen]

ΦΥΧΚ

[Σψμβολ]

COFFEE
TABLE ART

[Tahoma]

COFFEE TABLE

ART

[Tempus Sans ITC]

COFFEE
TABLE ART

[Times New Roman]

COFFEE

TABLE ART

[Trebuchet MS]

COFFEE TABLE

ART

[Tw Cen MT]

COFFEE TABLE

ART

[Tw Cen MT Condensed]

COFFEE TABLE ART

[Tw Cen MT Condensed Extra Bold]

COFFEE TABLE ART

[Verdana]

COFFEE
TABLE ART

[Viner Hand ITC]

COFFEE TABLE ART

[Vivaldi]

COFFEE TABLE ART

[Vladimir Script]

COFF EE TABL E ART

[Wide Latin]

COFFEE

TABLE ART

[Yu Gothic]

COFFEE
TABLE ART

[Yu Gothic Light]

COFFEE

TABLE ART

[Yu Gothic Medium]

COFFEE

TABLE ART

[Yu Gothic UI]

COFFEE TABLE

ART

[Yu Gothic UI Light]

COFFEE

TABLE ART

[Yu Gothic UI SemiBold]

COFFEE TABLE

ART

[Yu Gothic UI SemiLight]

COFFEE

TABLE ART

[Yu Mincho]